THE ECONOMIC EXPANSION OF THE 1990S

MARC LABONTE AND GAIL E. MAKINEN

Novinka Books
New York

Senior Editors: Susan Boriotti and Donna Dennis
Coordinating Editor: Tatiana Shohov
Office Manager: Annette Hellinger
Graphics: Wanda Serrano
Editorial Production: Vladimir Klestov, Matthew Kozlowski and Maya Columbus
Circulation: Ave Maria Gonzalez, Vera Popovic, Luis Aviles, Raymond Davis,
        Melissa Diaz and Jeannie Pappas
Communications and Acquisitions: Serge P. Shohov
Marketing: Cathy DeGregory

Library of Congress Cataloging-in-Publication Data

Labonte, Marc.
    The economic expansion of the 1990s / Marc Labonte and Gail E. Makinen.
      p. cm.
    Includes bibliographical references and index.
    ISBN 1-59033-458-2.
      1. Gross domestic product—United States—History—20th century. 2.
    United States—Economic conditions—1945-. I. Makinen, Gail E. II. Title.

HC110.I5 L267 2002
330.973'0929—dc21

                                              2002033653

Copyright © 2002 by Novinka Books, An Imprint of
      Nova Science Publishers, Inc.
      400 Oser Ave, Suite 1600
      Hauppauge, New York 11788-3619
      Tele. 631-231-7269   Fax 631-231-8175
      e-mail: Novascience@earthlink.net
      Web Site: http://www.novapublishers.com

Printed in the United States of America

CONTENTS

PREFACE

Of the ten economic expansions in the post-World War II era, three have been especially long: 1961-1969, 1982-1990, and 1991-2000. This study compares these three expansions in areas such as GDP growth, gross and net investment, growth and productivity of the labor force, the fiscal position of the federal government, and inflation. Such a comparison can provide perspective and insight into a number of perceived problems. Given the current economic turbulence we are facing, this book will serve as an important tool in studying the market cycle.

SUMMARY

The economic expansion that began in March 1991 is now the longest expansion in American history. The decisions by Congress concerning the disposition and use of the current and projected budget surpluses and timely action by the Federal Reserve, for which Congress has oversight responsibility, are likely to play important roles in the future directions of the economy

An economy's performance during an expansion can depend on the depth of the preceding downturn. Deep recessions are conductive to large gains in income growth and employment. The recession preceding the 1990s downturn was very shallow. This has had an influence on income growth, productivity gains, and declines in unemployment during the 1990s relative to the expansions of the 1960s and 1980s.

The major characteristics of the expansion of the 1990s, when compared to similar periods during the long expansions of the 1960s and 1980s, are that:

- It has the weakest growth in GDP; a growth heavily influenced by capital outlays. Government purchases have played a small role in the expansion.

- Net saving by the private sector has fallen sharply so that net investment has been sustained by the improved fiscal position of the federal government and a growing net inflow of foreign capital.

- Job growth, while large, is similar to the 80s and heavily concentrated in the service sector reflecting, in part, how Americans spend their incomes.

- The improved federal fiscal position has caused the national debt/GDP ratio to fall during the 90s compared to a rise in the 80s and fall in the 60s.

- The trend to a more open economy continues with the sum of exports and imports approaching 30% of GDP which is about 3 times larger than during the 1960s.

- Growth in the labor force was low. Productivity growth has been on the rise and is above the average for the 1980s.

- The inflation performance is favorable and parallels the early 1960s.

- Real gains from the Dow-Jones industrials and the S&P 500 are the largest of the three expansions.

- Gains in the per capita measures of material well-being are generally below the two other expansions, especially the 1960s. This is in line with the low productivity growth during the early part of the expansion.

Chapter 1

INTRODUCTION

In December 1998, the on-going economic expansion that began in March 1991 passed a major milestone: at 93 months it became both America's longest peacetime expansion and the second longest expansion in the recorded economic history of the United States. In February 2000 it passed another major milestone when it became the longest expansion in U.S. history.

Given its length, it is appropriate to compare it with two of its predecessors, the 92-month expansion that dominated the decade of the 1980s and the 106-month expansion that filled the decade of the 1960s.[1]

Such a comparison can provide perspective and insight into a number of currently perceived problems such as the nature of job creation, the state of public finances, the adequacy of the national saving and investment rates, the threat from inflation, the status of the balance of trade, the prospects for real economic growth and so on. These and other matters highlighted in the comparisons to follow may require the remedial attention of Congress if the on-going expansion (hereafter referred to as the 1990s expansion) is to continue. The comparisons also serve as a benchmark by which to judge the expansion of the 1990s. It may be that legislation can enhance the performance of the economy.

There are, of course, dangers in drawing sharp conclusions from comparisons spread over a nearly 40-year period. A number of structural

---

[1] The 1960s expansion began in February 1961 and lasted until December 1969. The 1980s expansion began in November 1982 and lasted until July 1990. The on-going expansion began in March 1991. The comparisons in this report will utilize data for the first seven

changes can occur in an economy that may make any comparisons of questionable value. These changes have occurred in the United States. The international monetary system, for example, moved from using fixed to flexible exchange rates. Additionally, the age/sex mix of the labor force changed, as did the extent and coverage of federal social insurance programs and the level and coverage of the federal minimum wage. These changes and others could be expected to affect the measure known as full employment. When these structural changes are thought to have an important influence on any conclusions, they will be noted.

Also of importance for the conclusions drawn in this study is the depth of the recession preceding the three expansions compared in this study. Frequently, attention is drawn to the fact that the recession preceding the expansion of the 1990s was very shallow compared with the two used for comparison purposes, especially the downturn running from July 1981 to November 1982. The latter is widely acknowledged as the most serious since the great depression. At various places in the discussion to follow, the influence of this shallow recession on the conclusions drawn from the comparisons with the two other expansions will be noted.

---

years or 84 months of each expansion. An epilogue contains additional comparisons of the 1980s and 1990s.

Chapter 2

THE GROWTH OF GDP AND ITS MAJOR COMPONENTS

The data on table 1 compares the three expansions studied in this report on the basis of how rapidly GDP grew each year and by its cumulative growth over the first seven years of the expansion.[1] In addition, the growth of the major components of GDP is also given. The reason is explained below.

The 1990s expansion turns in the weakest growth performance when a comparison is made on either an annual or cumulative basis. This is due primarily to two factors. First, this expansion began after a shallow recession. In 1991, the actual unemployment rate for the year, 6.7%, was only 0.8% above the Congressional Budget Office's (CBO) estimate of the full employment rate of unemployment, 5.9%. By way of contrast, the expansions of the 1960s and 1980s got under way with much more slack in the economy when the difference between the two unemployment rates was, respectively, 1.2% and 3.6%. Thus, in each of these expansions, GDP had more leeway to grow in order to achieve full employment. Second, productivity growth, which also effects how rapidly GDP can grow over the longer run, was considerably higher in the 1960s than after (see section below on productivity). This difference helps explain why such substantial growth was possible during the first 7 years of the 1960s expansion. Another way to view this is to look at the average annual growth rate of GDP over the

---

[1] This comparison uses a calendar year over calendar basis rather than using the first 12 months following the month or quarter in which the cyclical trough was reached. This alternative method could yield results that are slightly different on a year-by-year and cumulative basis.

first *seven* years of each expansion. The respective average rates for 1961-68, 1982-89, and 1991-98, were 5.2%, 4.3%, and 3.5%.

Perhaps the best way to measure the influence of both how fast GDP grew and its cumulative growth during these three expansions is to see how long it took full employment to be achieved in each expansion. This involves measuring how long it took the actual unemployment rate to converge on the unemployment rate that is compatible with full employment.[2] While the latter measure of unemployment is discussed below, for the present, only the number of quarters needed to achieve it will be noted. In the expansion of the 1990s, full employment was achieved in the 15th quarter out from the cyclical trough. In the 1980s, this took 19 quarters. The 1960s expansion furnishes mixed evidence. Full employment was achieved in the 5th quarter of the expansion (1962.2). Then, however, during most of 1963, the economy was initially at less than full employment, a situation remedied in 1964 (and beyond for the remainder of the expansion). Thus, in terms of the length of time needed to get to full employment, the expansion of the 1990s compares favorably with the two other expansions.

When the growth of the components of GDP is examined, the expansion of the 1990s is clearly led by investment spending. While the growth in this component of GDP has been important in each of the three expansions, it is relatively more important in the expansion of the 1990s. Over the period 1991-1998, the total growth in investment spending is some 3.3 times the total growth in GDP, which is more than twice as large as during the two other expansions.

Government spending, however, has played little role in the expansion of the 1990s. Real net spending by all levels of government has been virtually unchanged over the period 1991-1998. By way of contrast, government spending played a much more important role in the two other expansions studied in this report.

---

[2] As measured by the Non-accelerating Inflation Rate of Unemployment of NAIRU as computed by the Congressional Budget Office (January 2000).

**Table 1. The Growth of Real GDP and
Major Components (in percentages)**

	Years Out From Expansion Beginning[a]							
	1	2	3	4	5	6	7	Total over 7 years
Real GDP								
1991 Expansion	3.0	2.7	4.0	2.7	3.6	4.4	4.4	27.5
1982 Expansion	4.3	7.3	3.8	3.4	3.4	4.2	3.5	34
1961 Expansion	6	4.3	5.8	6.4	6.6	2.5	4.8	42.5
Consumption Component								
1991	2.9	3.4	3.8	3.0	3.2	3.6	4.7	27.1
1982	5.5	5.4	5	4.2	3.3	4	2.7	34.1
1961	4.9	4.1	6.0	6.3	5.7	3.0	5.7	41.7
Investment Component								
1991	8.5	8.7	13.2	3.0	9.0	12.1	12.5	88.8
1982	9.5	29.4	-0.9	-0.7	2.5	2.7	3.7	52.2
1961	12.7	6.7	8.3	14.0	8.8	-4.6	5.8	62.8
Government Component								
1991	0.5	-0.8	0.1	0.2	1.1	2.4	2.1	5.9
1982	3.3	3.5	6.4	5.4	3	1.2	2.8	28.4
1961	6.0	2.4	2.0	3.1	9.0	7.5	3.2	38.0

[a] The base year for measuring each expansion is, respectively, 1961, 1982, and 1991.
Source: Computed from data supplied by Department of Commerce.

CONSUMPTION

Since consumption expenditures comprise some two thirds of GDP, its major components are shown in table 2 for the three expansions.[3] Several things about these data should be noted. First, over the first 7 years of each expansion, the composition of consumption was remarkably stable. There was very little variation among its components. Thus, it is unlikely that changes in the composition of consumption are important for cyclical expansions. Second, over time, the composition of consumption has changed: nondurables are a decreasing fraction of the total while both services and durables are a rising fraction. This is the basis for the claim that the U.S. economy is becoming more service oriented. Several factors help explain these trends, such as the aging of the population, the growing

---

[3] The comparisons made in this table involve dividing the real value of the components of consumption by the real value of total consumption. Real values are also used for the computation on tables 4 and 8.

fraction of the labor force that consists of women, changes in technology, and increases in per capita income. Third, the changes in the composition of consumption are an important determinant of the type of jobs that are created in the economy.[4]

SAVING

The portion of the nation's output that is not used by the government and the private sector (for either consumption or capital goods), or sold to foreigners (less what is purchased from foreigners) represents what is termed saving. Saving is important because it represents the resources or output that is available to sustain and expand the national capital stock.[5]

Table 3 shows the sources of saving available to the United States. These sources are businesses, households (personal), governments, and from abroad. Gross saving is to be distinguished from net saving. A large portion of national saving comes from the depreciation allowances of businesses. This portion of saving is used to replace the capital stock worn out in the process of producing output. Net saving, on the other hand, represents the resources that are available to expand the capital stock to ensure that a growing labor force has the material means of production with which to work. In the private sector, net saving comes from the retained earnings of businesses and from the saving of households.

Net private saving is either augmented by the fiscal surpluses of the public sector or depleted by its fiscal deficits. Finally, net national saving can be augmented by a net inflow of foreign capital (saving) to the United States or decreased by a net capital outflow from the United States.

---

[4] For a more extensive discussion of the relationship between changes in the growth rate of the components of output and the nature of job creation, see CRS Report 96-988 E, *Job Creation in America: What Jobs Have Been Created and Why?* By Gail Makinen. December 9, 1996.

[5] For an extensive discussion of the concept of saving and U.S. saving behavior, see CRS Report 98-580 E, *Saving in the United States: Why it is Important and How Has it Changed.* By Brian Cashell and Gail Makinen. June 1, 1998.

Table 2. The Composition of Consumption (percentage distribution)

Expansion Years	Durables	Nondurables	Services
1992	11%	31%	57%
1993	12	31	58
1994	12	30	58
1995	12	30	58
1996	12	30	58
1997	12	30	58
1998	12	30	58
Expansion Average	12%	30%	58%
1983	13%	36%	51%
1984	13	35	52
1985	14	34	52
1986	14	33	53
1987	13	33	54
1988	13	32	54
1989	13	32	55
Expansion Average	13%	34%	53%
1962	13%	45%	42%
1963	14	44	43
1964	14	43	43
1965	14	43	43
1966	14	43	43
1967	14	43	43
1968	14	43	43
Expansion Average	14%	43%	43%

Source: Computed from data supplied by the Department of Commerce.

Table 3. Sources of U.S. Saving (percent of nominal GDP)

| Years | Business | | | Personal | Gross Private Sector[a] | Net Private Sector[b] | Government | | | Net National Saving[c] | Net Foreign Inflow[d] | Net Saving Available[e] |
	Retained Earnings	Capital Consumption Allowances	Total				Federal	S%L	Total			
1992	2.3	9.9	12.2	6.5	18.4	8.5	-3.5	1.0	-2.5	3.7	-0.6	4.3
1993	2.0	10.1	12.1	5.3	17.5	7.4	-2.9	1.1	-1.8	3.3	-1.1	4.4
1994	1.9	10.4	12.3	4.5	17.0	6.6	-1.9	1.2	-0.7	3.7	-1.5	5.2
1995	2.4	10.3	12.7	4.1	17.1	6.8	-1.5	1.3	-0.2	4.4	-1.3	5.7
1996	3.1	10.0	13.1	3.5	16.5	6.5	-0.7	1.4	0.7	5.0	-1.4	6.4
1997	3.2	10.0	13.2	3.3	16.5	6.5	0.4	1.5	1.9	6.2	-1.5	7.7
1998	3.1	9.9	13.0	2.6	15.6	5.6	1.5	1.6	3.1	4.6	-2.3	6.9
1983	2.6	10.6	13.2	6.4	19.6	9.0	-3.7	1.3	-2.4	4.2	-1.1	5.3
1984	2.4	10.7	13.1	7.8	21.0	10.9	-3.1	1.4	-1.4	7.2	-2.2	9.4
1985	2.9	10.2	13.1	6.7	19.8	9.1	-3.0	1.6	-1.4	5.4	-2.6	8.0
1986	1.8	10.2	12.0	6.0	18.1	7.9	-3.1	1.5	-1.6	4.1	-3.2	7.3
1987	2.2	10.1	12.3	5.3	17.7	7.5	-1.9	1.3	-0.6	4.7	-3.2	7.9
1988	2.7	10.1	12.8	5.7	18.5	8.4	-1.5	1.4	-0.1	6.0	-2.2	8.2
1989	1.9	10.0	11.9	5.5	17.4	7.3	-1.2	1.4	0.2	5.3	-1.6	6.9
1962	3.8	7.6	11.4	5.7	17.1	9.5	2.4	1.7	4.1	10.1	0.7	9.4
1963	4.1	7.4	11.5	5.3	16.8	9.4	2.8	1.8	4.6	11.2	0.8	10.4
1964	4.3	7.3	11.6	6.1	17.7	10.4	2.0	1.8	3.8	11.5	1.1	10.4
1965	4.8	7.2	12.0	5.9	18.0	10.7	2.2	1.8	4.0	12.0	0.9	11.1
1966	4.8	7.1	11.9	5.6	17.7	10.4	2.0	1.8	3.8	11.7	0.5	11.2
1967	4.2	7.4	11.6	6.5	18.1	10.7	0.7	1.7	2.4	10.5	0.4	10.1
1968	3.7	7.4	11.1	5.8	16.9	9.5	1.5	1.7	3.2	10.2	0.2	10.0

[a] Gross Private Sector = Total Business saving + Personal Saving [b] Net Private Sector = Retained Earnings + Personal Saving
[c] Net National Saving = Net Private Sector Saving + Net Government Saving (or Gross Government Savings less capital consumption allowance)
[d] Negative numbers mean an inflow of foreign saving to the United States while positive numbers mean an outflow of U.S. saving to foreign countries
[e] Net Saving Available = Net National Saving + Net Foreign Inflow (add negative number to total; subtract positive number from total)
Source: Computed from data supplied by the Department of Commerce

The saving behavior of Americans is markedly different over these three economic expansions. In fact, the expansions may be capturing what is, in effect, a secular trend. In summary these differences are:

- total or gross private sector saving has averaged a smaller fraction of GDP during the 1990s expansion than during the two other expansions (about 3.5% to 11% less).

- net private sector saving, a major source for additions to the capital stock, was highest during the expansion of the 1960s. It has declined over each successive expansion. During the 1990s it was, on average, about 33% below the average of the 1960s.

- the fall in net private sector saving between the 1960s and 1990s is due to a nearly 27% fall in the average personal saving rate and about a 40% fall in the average retained earnings rate. Particularly disquieting is the decline in the household saving rate during 1998 and 1999. In 1998, it averaged about 2.6% of GDP while during 1999 it was less than 2%.[6]

- the average net national saving rate has declined from 11.0% of GDP during the 1960s to 4.4% of GDP during the 1990s – a fall of nearly 60%.

- the decline in the average net national saving rate, in addition to the decline in the net private sector saving rate, is due to a sharp decline in the fiscal surpluses of the public sector (all levels of government). This has been a decline from an average surplus of about 1.0% of GDP during the 1960s to –1.9% during the 1990s.[7]

- the total net saving available to the United States (from both domestic and foreign sources) has declined from an average of 10.4% of GDP during the 1960s to 5.8% during the 1990s – a fall of about 44%. This decline was not as large as the decline in average net national saving because of net foreign capital movements. During the 1960s, the U.S. sent capital abroad which, on an annual basis, averaged about 0.7% of GDP. During the 1990s, the U.S. absorbed foreign saving or capital that averaged, on an annual basis, about 1.6% of GDP.

---

[6] For a discussion of the collapse of household saving, see CRS Report RS20224, *The Collapse of Household Saving: Why Has It Happened and What are its Implications?*, by Brian W. Cashell and Gail E. Makinen.

[7] Over the course of the 1990s, the fiscal position of the federal government steadily improved. The average for the entire period, which is negative, conceals this improvement.

Overall, developments concerning U.S. saving rates have raised serious questions. The U.S. private sector is saving a smaller and smaller fraction of GDP in each expansion. The U.S. public sector fiscal surplus (or saving) has declined from an average of about 1.0% of GDP per year to an average of about −1.9% per year and domestic investment has tended to depend increasingly on foreign saving. There are some surprises in these developments. An important one is that the rate of productivity growth has not only not declined as one might have expected given the decline in the net national saving rate and the rate of net saving available to the United States, but actually appears to be regaining the rate last seen in the 1960s.

GROSS PRIVATE DOMESTIC INVESTMENT

It was noted above that the expansion of the 1990s is, so to speak, investment led. The data in table 4 show that the composition of fixed investment during the 1990s expansion is quite different from the two other expansions. The difference, however, appears to be part of a secular trend. These data show that the capital allocated to structures and residential investment has declined over the past 35 years as a fraction of total fixed investment while the proportion due to producers durable equipment has risen from about 40% of the total during the 1960s to about 55% during the 1990s.

When the producers' durable equipment category is further subdivided, it can be seen that a large portion of the total during both the 1980s and 1990s expansions is accounted for by "information procession and related equipment." During the 1980s, this was 66% of the total outlay for Producers' Durable Equipment while during the 1990s it was 68% of the total.[8]

While gross investment is important to the level and growth of GDP and employment, it is not totally relevant to the long run sustainable rate of growth of the economy and to improvements in the material well-being of the population. This depends on net investments (or gross investment less depreciation) for it is net investment that adds to the capital stock of the country. Table 5 records the growth of net investment over the three expansions compared in this report.

---

[8] By way of contrast, total outlays for this component was about 9% of Producers' Durable Equipment during the expansion of the 1960s.

Table 4. Composition of Gross Domestic Fixed Investment (percentage of total fixed investment)

Expansion Years	Structures	Nonresidential Producers' Durable Equipment	Residential
1992	20.2%	53.3%	26.5%
1993	19.2	53.8	27.0
1994	18.1	54.2	27.6
1995	18.4	55.9	25.7
1996	18.6	55.6	25.8
1997	19.3	56.0	24.7
1998	19.2	56.0	24.8
Expansion Average	18.9%	54.9%	26.1%
1983	26.8%	46.4%	26.8%
1984	26.3	46.9	26.8
1985	27.1	46.8	26.2
1986	23.7	46.8	29.4
1987	22.8	47.0	30.2
1988	22.6	48.2	29.2
1989	22.9	49.7	27.4
Expansion Average	24.6%	47.4%	28.0%
1962	25.3%	39.3%	35.3%
1963	24.1	39.5	36.4
1964	24.4	40.3	35.3
1965	26.0	42.7	31.4
1966	26.6	45.9	27.5
1967	26.5	46.2	27.3
1968	25.4	45.3	29.3
Expansion Average	25.5%	42.8%	31.8%

Source: Computed from data supplied by the Department of Commerce.

Table 5. Net Domestic Investment and GDP* (as a percentage of GDP)

| | Years Out From Trough | | | | | | | |
Expansion	1	2	3	4	5	6	7	Expansion Average
1992-98	3.3	4.4	5.5	5.6	6.3	7.0	NA	5.2
1983-89	5.2	8.6	7.5	6.7	6.4	5.9	5.8	6.6
1961-68	7.4	7.6	8.0	9.2	9.4	7.9	8.0	8.2

Source: Computed from data supplied by the Department of Commerce.
* Nominal Net Domestic Investment divided by nominal GDP.

Most observers do not find these results reassuring. The average expansion of net domestic investment during the 1990s has declined by about 1/3 on average relative to the 1960s and by 1/5 on average from the 1980s. This should come as no surprise since saving governs the resources available for investment in the economy. And, as noted in table 3, net saving available has declined across time when the 1990s are compared with the 1960s.

The longer run implications of the falling rate of net domestic fixed investment are mitigated to some degree by a decline in the growth rate of the labor force. When labor force growth declines, the capital/labor ratio can be sustained with a reduced growth rate of net investment.[9]

---

[9] One other aspect of this decline in the growth rate of fixed net investment should be noted. A large fraction of the new **additional** capital put in place is either directly or indirectly foreign owned – the byproduct of the U.S. being the recipient of a net inflow of foreign capital. Thus, the reward payable to this capital accrues to foreigners. For this reason, it is possible for U.S. GDP to grow while a smaller and smaller portion of that growth accrues to American.

Chapter 3

THE STATE OF PUBLIC FINANCES

It is not unusual to see a large federal budget deficit during the initial stage of an economic expansion. The deficit may reflect both the lingering effects of the depressed state of the economy and any application of counter-cyclical fiscal policy. It has, however, been the American experience to see the deficit decline as a fraction of GDP as an expansions matures.

The desired magnitude of the decline in the deficit over an expansion is, however, contentious. There are economists who believe that the budget should be balanced when the economy is at full employment. There are others who argue that it should be balanced on average over the cycle meaning that budget deficits are fully offset by surpluses. This line of reasoning implies that when the economy is at full employment, the budget should be in surplus not just in balance.[1]

The public finance experience of the United States over the three expansions compared in this report is recorded in summary form on table 6. The year in which full employment is achieved is relevant to an assessment of this experience. That year, based on CBO data, is indicated by an *.[2]

Table 6 also reports the structural budget deficit, or deficit that would occur if the economy were at full employment. Shifts in this deficit as a percent of potential or full employment GDP are thought to provide a better

---

[1] Various methods exist to compute the federal budget deficit. See CRS Report 94-637 E, *Measuring the Federal Budget Deficit*, by Brian W. Cashell, Library of Congress, Washington, DC: August 3, 1994.

[2] The relevant CBO data is its measure of NAIRU or the rate of unemployment compatible with full employment. During the expansion of the 1960s, the actual unemployment rate dipped below the NAIRU in 1962, rose above it in 1963 and, then, fell below it in 1964. During the expansion of the 1980s, full employment was not achieved until 1987.

signal of the posture of fiscal policy than is provided by movements in the actual deficit relative to actual GDP.

Comparing structural deficits as a percentage of potential or full employment GDP leads to the conclusion that the 1990s were a period of substantial fiscal tightening compared to the 1980s and 1960s. The 1960s, by this measure, was a period of fiscal expansion. The 1980s stand out as the only period since 1945 where large structural deficits were maintained for several years.

Table 6. Federal Budget Deficit and GDP[a] (in percentages)

Expansion Years	Budget Deficit as a Percentage of GDP	Structural Deficit/ Potential GDP
1992	4.7%	3.0%
1993	3.9	2.6
1994	2.9	2.0
1995	2.2*	1.9
1996	1.4	1.2
1997	0.3	0.9
1998	-0.8	0.4
Expansion Average	2.0%	2.2%
1983	6.0%	3.2%
1984	4.8	3.7
1985	5.1	4.3
1986	5.0	4.8
1987	3.2*	3.4
1988	3.1	2.6
1989	2.8	2.2
Expansion Average	3.4%	3.9%
1962	1.3%	0.6%
1963	0.8	0.5
1964	0.9*	0.8
1965	0.2	0.5
1966	0.5	1.6
1967	1.1	2.4
1968	2.9	3.4
Expansion Average	1.1%	1.7%

[a] The federal budget deficit is on a NIPA basis.
Source: Computed from data supplied by the Congressional Budget Office.
* Full employment reached.

The budget deficit fell as a fraction of GDP during both the expansions of the 1980s and 1990s.[3] During the 1960s, the small budget surplus gave way to a deficit under the pressure of the Vietnam War. Interestingly, in the seventh year of the 1990s expansion, the budget deficit gave way to a surplus whereas in the final year of the expansion of the 1980s the deficit was still nearly 3% of GDP.

Misleading conclusions can be drawn from a comparison of the ratio of the budget deficit to GDP during the 1990s compared with the 1980s. The fact that they are smaller in the 1990s is due in part to the fact that the economic downturn that preceded the 1980s expansion was the deepest contraction in the post-World War II era. The 1990-91 contraction was, by way of contrast, very shallow. Thus, the deficit/GDP ratio during the 1980s should have been larger than during the 1990s. A better comparison comes from the comparison of structural deficits, with reveals that the deficits of the 1980s were still much larger than those of the 1990s.

The ratio of the interest-bearing national debt to GDP is frequently used by economists as a measure of the burden of a national debt to a nation's economy.[4] A rising ratio is regarded as an increasing burden. While this does not imply that there is some magic number at which the burden becomes unbearable, it does mean that over the longer run the policy can become unsustainable – a public debt cannot grow faster than the growth of GDP forever. Ultimately, history shows, governments caught in such a bind have resorted to printing money to finance their budget deficits. While the United States is nowhere near such a situation today, a growing public debt to GDP ratio can be a sign of trouble to come.[5]

---

[3] Generally accepted macroeconomic theory suggests that, when the currencies of countries are linked via flexible exchange rates and where capital mobility is high, changes in trade deficits should go hand-in-hand with changes in budget deficits (measured as the full employment or structural deficits) assuming that **all else is held constant**. This linkage was strong during the 1980s. It has not been strong during the 1990s. In fact, the reverse is true: a rising trade deficit has been going hand-in-hand with a falling structural (and actual) budget deficit. For a discussion of this relationship, see CRS Report 96-112 E, *As the Budget Deficit Is Reduced, What Happens to the Foreign Trade Deficit?*, by Gail Makinen, Library of Congress, Washington, DC: February 1, 1996, CRS Report 97-985 E, Why the Budget Deficit and the Trade Deficit Haven't Been Moving Together. By Gail Makinen. April 19, 2000.

[4] The non-interest bearing debt of the United States consists of currency and coin in circulation. It is not included in the national debt calculations used in this paper.

[5] A more complete discussion of the burden of a nation debt can be found in CRS Report RL30520, The National Debt: Who Bears its Burden? By Gail Makinen. April 7, 2000; see also CRS Report 95-996 E, *The Economic Effects of a Large Federal Debt*. By Brian W. Cashell. September 22, 1995, and CRS Report RL30583, *The Economics of the Federal Budget Surplus*. By Brian W. Cashell. June 20, 2000.

For comparison purposes, it should be recalled that at the end of World War II, the United States had a national debt larger than its GDP, i.e.; the ratio was greater than 1.0.

While the national debt/GDP ratio rose during the first five years of the expansion of the 1990s, the movement of the federal budget toward surplus as well as the growth in GDP has caused the ratio to fall over the last two years. The ratio fell during the expansion of the 1960s and rose during the expansion of the 1980s.

Table 7. National Debt and GDP

Expansion Years	National Debt as a Percentage of GDP
1992	64.3%
1993	66.3
1994	66.8
1995	67.2
1996	67.3
1997	65.5
1998	63.2
1983	39.9%
1984	40.7
1985	43.9
1986	48.2
1987	50.4
1988	51.9
1989	53.0
1962	53.3%
1963	51.7
1964	49.2
1965	46.8
1966	43.4
1967	41.9
1968	42.4

Source: Computed from data supplied by the Departments of Commerce and Treasury.

Chapter 4

THE EXTERNAL SECTOR

When Americans drink their morning coffee they are reminded early every day that we do not produce all that we consume. In fact, a noticeable trend in the post-World War II era is the increasing openness of the U.S. economy as measured by the fraction of GDP accounted for by the sum of what is exported and imported. This increasing openness is one of the developments shown in table 8.

Over the past 35 years, the sum of exports and imports has risen from less than 10% to 25% of GDP. Given the size of the U.S. economy, America has become a major market for many foreign countries. And, increasingly, the world market is of growing importance for many American firms.

A second interesting piece of information from table 8 are the data on net exports. A common feature of these three expansions is a trade deficit, although the relative magnitude of the deficit increased during the 1990s relative to the two earlier expansions.

The largest trade deficits, in both absolute and relative to GDP, occurred during 1998. The United States received an inflow of foreign capital (or foreign saving) equal to 3.2% of GDP. During 1999 this had increased to about 4% of GDP.[1]

Economic theory suggests that the behavior of the trade deficit during the 1960s expansion should be somewhat different from the two other focus expansions because during that period the United States maintained fixed exchange rates between the dollar and other currencies.

---

[1] For a discussion of the causes and effects of the U.S. trade deficit, see CRS Report RL30532, *America's Growing Current Account Deficit: Its Causes and What It Means for the Economy*. By Gail Makinen. April 19, 2000.

Table 8. Foreign Trade and GDP (billions of 1992 dollars)

	Net Exports			
Expansion Years	1996 Dollars	Percentage of GDP	Exports and Imports as a Percent of GDP	Growth in Exports
1992	-$19.8	0.3%	19.2%	6.2%
1993	-59.1	0.8	19.9	3.3
1994	-86.6	1.2	21.1	8.9
1995	-78.4	1.0	22.5	10.3
1996	-88.9	1.1	23.5	8.2
1997	-113.3	1.4	25.4	12.5
1998	-221.0	2.5	25.1	2.2
Expansion Average	-$95.3	1.2	22.4	63.8*
1983	-$63.8	1.2%	13.2%	-2.4%
1984	-128.4	2.3	14.4	8.4
1985	-149.1	2.6	14.6	2.7
1986	-165.1	2.8	15.2	7.4
1987	-156.2	2.6	15.9	11.2
1988	-112.1	1.8	16.6	16.1
1989	-79.4	1.2	17.3	11.8
Expansion Average	-$122.0	2.1	15.3	68.3*
1962	-$25.8	1.0%	8.3%	5.4%
1963	-22.0	0.8	8.3	7.5
1964	-15.0	0.5	8.6	13.4
1965	-26.4	0.9	8.6	0.2
1966	-39.9	1.2	8.9	6.7
1967	-49.2	1.5	9.2	2.2
1968	-66.1	1.9	9.8	7.3
Expansion Average	-$34.9	1.1	8.8	53.3*

Source: Computed from data supplied by the Department of Commerce.
* Expansion total.

In a fixed exchange rate world, fiscal expansion would put upward pressure on U.S. interest rates, attracting foreign capital. This increased desire by foreigners to purchase dollars to buy American assets would put upward pressure on the exchange rate. To prevent the dollar from rising in value or appreciating (a requirement of a fixed exchange rate), the Federal Reserve would have to increase the supply of dollars (or money). This would, in turn, keep U.S. interest rates from rising as high as they would have otherwise.

Because dollar appreciation would have been prevented by Federal Reserve action, the fiscal expansion would not have led to a foreign trade deficit of the same magnitude as would have occurred if flexible exchange rates were used.

Chapter 5

LABOR PRODUCTIVITY, JOB CREATION, AND UNEMPLOYMENT

Increases in the rate at which labor productivity grows is another way to measure the growth in the American standard of living. In some ways it is a better measure than GDP growth because it accounts for some of the effort Americans put into producing output.

The growth in labor productivity tends to vary with the cycle, rising in the early phase of each expansion.[1] An increase that is sustained over a period of years is clearly significant and unlikely to be a purely cyclical phenomenon.

The U.S. labor productivity experience over the three expansions compared in this report is shown in table 9. These data reveal a now widely acknowledged development – the market decline in productivity growth that became noticeable beginning in the early 1970s.

The 1990s economic expansion has a most interesting pattern of labor productivity growth. Because the 1990-91 recession was shallow, rapid productivity growth over the first several years of the expansion was not expected. And, indeed, it did not occur. Essentially, there was only one good year of productivity growth, 1992. Beginning in 1996, however, the growth rate of labor productivity began to rise, averaging about 2.4% per year for

---

[1] This occurs because layoffs in the downswing of the cycle seldom reflect precisely any decline in production by a firm. Thus, in the upswing, output or production can be increased initially with little or no additional input of labor. The net result is a rise in "output per hour of all persons" or labor productivity.

three years. (As noted in the Epilogue, productivity growth continued at a rapid pace during 1999 and the first half of 2000.)[2]

Table 9. Labor Productivity (percent change)

Expansion Years	Labor Productivity	
	Business Sector	Nonfarm Business Sector
1992	3.9%	3.7%
1993	0.5	0.5
1994	1.3	1.3
1995	0.7	0.9
1996	2.8	2.5
1997	2.1	1.8
1998	2.7	2.6
Expansion Average	2.0%	1.9%
1983	3.6%	4.5%
1984	2.8	2.2
1985	2.0	1.3
1986	3.0	3.0
1987	0.5	0.4
1988	1.2	1.3
1989	1.0	0.8
Expansion Average	2.0%	1.9%
1962	4.6%	4.5%
1963	3.9	3.5
1964	4.6	4.2
1965	3.6	3.1
1966	4.1	3.5
1967	2.2	1.7
1968	3.1	3.1
Expansion Average	3.7%	3.4%

Source: Computed from data supplied by the Department of Labor.

While the decline in productivity growth that became noticeable in the early 1970s remains largely unexplained, some economists link it to various

---

[2] For a discussion of productivity during the expansion of the 1990s, see CRS Report RL30158, *Productivity Growth in the Current Economic Expansion: A Comparative Analysis*, by Brian W. Cashell, Library of Congress, Washington, DC: April 29, 1999.

changes that have occurred in employment patterns. As shown in table 10, job growth has been increasingly concentrated in the service sector where it is difficult to measure "output per hour of all persons," the official name for productivity. Part of the decline may also be due to the changed composition of the labor force, especially the increasing proportion of the work force composed of younger workers whose productivity is thought to be lower than that of more mature and seasoned workers.[3]

There are several interesting facets to the data in table 10. First, they show that in terms of the absolute increase in employment and employment increases by sector, the expansion of the 1980s and 1990s are quite similar. In relative terms, however, the employment increases during the 1980s were substantially larger. For example, while employment increased 17.2 million over the period 1992-98 and 17.7 million during 1983-89, in terms of percentage increases the figures for the two periods are 15.8% vs. 19.6%. This is in contrast to a 22.3% increase during the expansion of the 1960s. Second, during all three of these expansions, the vast majority of jobs were created in the service sector: 73% in the 1960s, 89% in the 1980s, and 88% in the 1990s. Third, during the 1980s and 1990s there was little job growth in the manufacturing sector while job growth in this sector during the 1960s accounted for 23% of the total. Fourth, job growth in the public sector has been confined to state and local governments especially during the 1990s when total federal employment declined.[4]

Along with major changes in the nature of job creation have come various changes in the work force. These changes are detailed in table 11.

As might be expected, these data show that as expansions continue, the unemployment rate declines. The early years of the expansion of the 1990s were atypical in that the unemployment rate continued to rise throughout the first year of the recovery.[5]

The 45% decline in the unemployment rate over the 1980s was the largest of these three expansions. During the 1990s, the relative fall was 39%

---

[3] The baby boomers who entered the labor force in great numbers during the 1970s are now part of the growing group of mature workers. Their maturation may help explain the rise in productivity growth. The median age of the labor force in 1998 is now the same as in the

[4] There is a tendency to focus public policy on job creation. For a well reasoned alternative, see CRS Report 92-697 E, *Is Job Creation a Meaningful Policy Justification?*, by Jane Gravelle, Don Kiefer, and Dennis Zimmerman, Library of Congress, Washington, DC: September 8, 1992.

[5] This atypical behavior may be related to corporate downsizing. The staff cuts announced by American companies were beginning to increase noticeably in the early years of the expansion of the 1990s. For a discussion of corporate downsizing and the related phenomenon of job insecurity, see CRS Report 96-175 E, *Corporate Downsizing: Labor*

whilst during the 1960s it was 35%. This ordering is due in part to the severity of the downturn that preceded the expansion of the 1980s.

All three expansions share in common the fact that by their seventh year the actual unemployment rates were below the CBO estimates of the NAIRU. This means that, based on the NAIRU measure of full employment, each expansion was experiencing excess demand by its seventh year.[6]

For the unemployment rate to fall during an economic expansion jobs not only have to be found for the unemployed, but for the new entrants into the labor force and for any net increase in the fraction of the population that want to work.

The percentage growth in the civilian labor force over the expansion of the 1990s has been the smallest of the three focus expansions with a growth rate of 7.5% versus 11.0% during the 1980s and 11.5% during the 1960s.[7] The decline in labor force growth in the 1990s reflects mainly declining fertility patterns in the United States over the past 20 years. In addition, the percentage growth in the ratio of civilian employment to the civilian non-institutional population (the Employment Ratio) is only about one-half of the growth rate registered during the 1980s (4.4% versus 8.8%), although it is larger than during the 1960s (4.4% versus 3.6%).

Market Aspects, by Linda Levine, Library of Congress, Washington, DC: updated regularly; and CRS Report RL30263, *Pension Policy: The Connection to Job Stability*

[6] For a discussion of NAIRU and why it changes over time, see CRS Report 94-748 E, *What is the Natural Rate of Unemployment?*, by Brian W. Cashell, Library of Congress, Washington, DC: September 16, 1994.

[7] The so-called baby boom generation entered the labor market during the 1970s. The labor force grew some 19.6% during a comparable part of that decade.

Table 10. Employment by Sector[a] (data in millions)

					Major Industries											
		Goods Producing Industries						Service Producing Industries						Government		
				Manufacturing												
	Total	Total	Mining	Construc-tion	Total	Durable	Non-Durable	Total	Trans & Public Utilities	Whole-SaleTrade	Retail Trade	Finance Insurance & Real Estate	Services	Total	Federal	State & Local
1992	108.6	23.2	0.6	4.5	18.1	10.3	7.8	85.4	5.7	6.0	19.4	6.6	29.1	18.6	3.0	15.7
1993	110.7	23.4	0.6	4.7	18.1	10.2	7.9	87.4	5.8	6.0	19.8	6.8	30.2	18.8	2.9	15.9
1994	114.2	23.9	0.6	5.0	18.3	10.4	7.9	90.3	6.0	6.2	20.5	6.9	31.6	19.1	2.9	16.3
1995	117.2	24.3	0.6	5.2	18.5	10.7	7.8	92.9	6.1	6.4	21.2	6.8	33.1	19.3	2.8	16.5
1996	119.6	24.5	0.6	5.4	18.5	10.8	7.7	95.1	6.3	6.5	21.6	6.9	34.5	19.4	2.8	16.7
1997	122.7	25.0	0.6	5.7	18.7	11.0	7.7	97.8	6.4	6.6	22.0	7.1	36.0	19.6	2.7	16.9
1998	125.8	25.3	0.5	6.0	18.8	11.2	7.6	100.5	6.6	6.8	22.3	7.4	3705	19.8	2.7	17.1
Net Change	17.2	2.1	-0.1	1.5	0.7	0.9	-0.2	15.1	0.9	0.8	2.9	0.8	8.4	0.9	-0.3	1.4
1983	90.2	23.3	1.0	3.9	18.4	10.7	7.7	66.8	5.0	5.3	15.6	5.5	19.7	15.8	2.8	13.1
1984	94.4	24.7	1.0	4.4	19.4	11.5	7.9	69.7	5.2	5.6	16.5	5.7	20.7	16.0	2.8	13.2
1985	97.4	24.8	0.9	4.7	19.2	11.5	7.8	72.5	5.2	5.7	17.3	5.9	21.9	16.4	2.9	13.5
1986	99.3	24.5	0.8	4.8	18.9	11.2	7.8	74.8	5.2	5.8	17.9	6.3	23.0	16.7	2.9	13.8
1987	102.0	24.7	0.7	5.0	19.0	11.2	7.8	77.3	5.4	5.8	18.4	6.5	24.1	17.0	2.9	14.1
1988	1.05.2	25.1	0.7	5.1	19.3	11.4	8.0	80.7	5.5	6.0	19.0	6.6	25.5	17.4	3.0	14.4
1989	107.9	25.3	0.7	5.2	19.4	11.4	8.0	82.6	5.6	6.2	19.5	6.7	26.9	17.8	3.0	14.8
Net Change	17.7	2.0	-0.3	1.3	1.0	0.7	0.3	15.8	0.6	0.9	3.9	1.2	7.2	2.0	0.2	1.7
1962	55.5	20.5	0.7	2.9	16.9	9.5	7.4	35.1	3.9	3.2	8.4	2.8	8.0	8.9	2.3	6.6
1963	56.7	20.6	0.6	3.0	17.0	9.6	7.4	36.0	3.9	3.3	8.5	2.8	8.3	9.2	2.4	6.9
1964	58.3	21.0	0.6	3.1	17.3	9.8	7.5	37.3	4.0	3.3	8.8	2.9	8.7	9.6	2.3	7.2
1965	60.8	21.9	0.6	3.2	18.1	10.4	7.7	38.8	4.0	3.5	9.2	3.0	9.0	10.0	2.4	7.7

		Major Industries															
	Goods Producing Industries						Service Producing Industries									
				Manufacturing											Government	
Total	Total	Mining	Construc-tion	Total	Durable	Non-Durable	Total	Trans & Public Utilities	Whole-SaleTrade	Retail Trade	Finance Insurance & Real Estate	Services	Total	Federal	State & Local
1966	63.9	23.2	0.6	3.3	19.2	11.3	8.0	40.7	4.2	3.6	9.6	3.0	9.5	10.8	2.6	8.2
1967	65.8	23.3	0.6	3.3	19.4	11.4	8.0	42.5	4.3	3.7	9.9	3.2	10.0	11.4	2.7	8.7
1968	67.9	23.7	0.6	3.4	19.8	11.6	8.2	44.2	4.3	3.8	10.3	3.3	10.6	11.8	2.7	9.1
Net Change	12.4	3.2	-0.1	0.5	2.9	2.1	0.8	9.1	0.4	0.6	1.9	0.5	2.6	2.9	0.4	2.5

Source: Department of Labor

Table 11. The Unemployment Rate and Employment Rates (data in percentages)

| Expansion Years | Civilian Unemployment Rate | NAIRU[c] | Employment Rate[a] | Labor Force Growth Rate | Labor Force Participation Rate[b] | | | |
					Male	Female	Both Sexes 16-19 Years	All Civilian Workers
1992	7.4%	5.7%	61.4%	1.4%	76.5%	57.7%	51.3%	66.3%
1993	6.8	5.6	61.6	0.9	76.2	58.0	51.5	66.2
1994	6.1	5.4	62.5	1.4	75.9	58.9	52.7	66.6
1995	5.6	5.3	62.9	1.0	75.7	59.0	53.5	66.6
1996	5.4	5.2	63.2	1.2	75.8	59.1	52.3	66.8
1997	4.9	5.2	63.8	1.8	75.9	59.5	51.6	67.1
1998	4.5	5.2	64.1	1.0	75.6	59.4	52.8	67.1

Expansion Years	Civilian Unemployment Rate	NAIRU[c]	Employment Rate[a]	Labor Force Growth Rate	Labor Force Participation Rate[b]			
					Male	Female	Both Sexes 16-19 Years	All Civilian Workers
1983	9.6%	6.1%	57.9%	1.2%	77.1%	52.7%	53.5%	64.0%
1984	7.5	6.1	59.5	1.8	77.1	53.3	53.9	64.4
1985	7.2	6.0	60.1	1.7	77.0	5401	54.5	64.8
1986	7.0	6.0	60.7	2.1	76.9	55.0	54.7	65.3
1987	6.2	6.0	61.5	1.7	76.8	55.7	54.7	65.6
1988	5.5	5.9	62.3	1.5	76.9	56.4	55.3	65.9
1989	5.3	5.9	63.0	1.8	77.1	57.2	55.9	66.5
1962	5.5%	5.5%	55.5%	0.2%	82.1%	36.7%	46.1%	58.8%
1963	5.7	5.5	55.4	1.7	81.5	37.2	45.2	58.7
1964	5.2	5.6	55.7	1.8	81.1	37.5	44.5	58.7
1965	4.5	5.6	56.2	1.9	80.8	38.1	45.7	58.9
1966	3.8	5.7	56.9	1.8	80.6	39.2	48.2	59.2
1967	3.8	5.8	57.3	2.1	80.6	40.1	48.4	59.6
1968	3.6	5.8	57.5	1.8	80.4	40.7	48.3	59.6

[a] The ratio of civilian employment to civilian non-institutional population.
[b] The ratio of the civilian labor force (employed plus unemployed) to civilian non-institutional population.
Source: Computed from data supplied by Department of Commerce.
[c] NAIRU is taken from CBO (January 2000)

These data also show a major trend in the United States – the decline in the labor force participation rate to men and the dramatic rise in this rate for women. This shift is unrelated to cyclical movements.[8]

---

[8] The rise in the labor force participation rate and the employment rate have implications for economic growth and increases in real per capita income. Economic growth comes not only from growth in the labor force due to population growth, but also from growth in the fraction of the population that wants to work. This latter force adding to growth is, of course, limited. Once the entire adult civilian population is employed, only population growth itself can add to potential income growth. However, in the interim, as individuals in the existing population change status from not working to working, measured output will rise for a given population pushing up per capita income.

Chapter 6

Inflation, the Inflation/ Unemployment Tradeoff, and Inflation Acceleration

Historical evidence suggests to many observers that a major reason economic expansions have come to an end is that policymakers have taken action to bring down what they regarded as an unacceptable rate of inflation. In table 12 the inflation experience of the three expansions compared in this report is reported using a price index from the GDP accounts, the Consumer Price Index, and the Producer Price Index (for finished goods).

From the perspective of both the annual increase in the rate of inflation and the cumulative rise in the price level, the expansions of the 1960s and the 1990s turn in a better performance that the 1980s. This relative performance helps put to rest the belief held by some economists that inflation is conductive to economic growth. During these three expansions, the highest rate goes hand-in-hand with the lowest inflation rate.

The data in tables 11 and 12 permit two other interesting comparisons. Looking first at the expansion of the 1960s, the data reveal that a trade off existed between the rate of inflation and the unemployment rate. That is, as the unemployment rate fell, the inflation rate tended to accelerate. Many economists of the time made a great deal about this tradeoff. Others were less sanguine since the result, if permanent, appeared to be inconsistent with a long held view that money is neutral in its ability to alter the state of the real variables in the economy. According to this view, changes in the growth rate of the money supply can change the rate of inflation, money wages, and market interest rates but it cannot changes relative prices, real wages, and the real interest rate, all factors that determine employment and output growth.

Table 12. The Rate of Inflation (data in percentages)

Expansion Years	Chain-Type GDP Deflator	Consumer Price Index	Producer Price Index
1992	2.4%	3.0%	1.2%
1993	2.4	3.0	1.2
1994	2.1	2.6	0.6
1995	2.2	2.8	1.9
1996	1.9	3.0	2.7
1997	1.9	2.3	0.4
1998	1.3	1.6	-0.9
Percentage Rise in the Price Level 1991-98	15.0%	19.7%	7.3%
1983	3.9%	3.2%	1.6%
1984	3.7	4.3	2.1
1985	3.2	3.6	1.0
1986	2.2	1.9	-1.4
1987	3.0	3.6	2.1
1988	3.4	4.1	2.5
1989	3.8	4.8	5.2
Percentage Rise in the Price Level 1982-89	25.7%	28.5%	13.6%
1962	1.4%	1.0%	0.3%
1963	1.1	1.3	-0.3
1964	1.5	1.3	0.3
1965	1.9	1.6	1.8
1966	2.8	2.9	3.2
1967	3.1	3.1	1.1
1968	4.3	4.2	2.8
Percentage Rise in the Price Level 1961-68	17.2%	16.4%	9.5%

Source: Computed from data supplied by the Department of Commerce.

The tradeoff pattern is not so evident in the expansions of the 1980s and 1990s. During the 1990s, both the inflation rate and the unemployment rate have declined. During the first four years of the expansion of the 1980s, both rates declined. During the following three years, however, the tradeoff pattern emerged.[1]

The second point worth investigating is how long it takes from the time the actual unemployment falls below the NAIRU until the inflation rate begins to accelerate. This has not occurred during the expansion of the 1990s even though the actual rate has been below the CBO's estimate of the NAIRU for at least three years. During the 1980s, the data suggest that it took about 2 years for the inflation rate to accelerate. A firm conclusion is somewhat difficult for the 1960s expansion since the actual unemployment rate was initially at the NAIRU, then above it and, finally, in the third year of the expansion, below it. If we take the third year as the starting point, it took about 2 years before the inflation rate began to accelerate. Based on only two prior observations, the behavior of the inflation rate during the expansion of the 1990s appears to be atypical.

From the perspective of both the rate of inflation and the total rise in the price level, the expansions of the 1960s and 1990s turn in a better performance than the 1980s.

---

[1] See CRS Report RL30391. *Inflation and Unemployment: What is the Connection?* By Brian W. Cashell. December 17, 1999.

Chapter 7

IMPROVEMENTS IN
MATERIAL WELL-BEING

The data in table 13 are designed to measure movements in the material well-being of Americans. Three measures, "Real Disposable Income Per Capita," "Real GDP Per Capita," and "Real Compensation Per Hour" are used in this comparison.

Of these three expansions, the 1990s has the weakest gain in material well-being. The rise in Real Disposable Personal Income Per Capita is about 1/3 the gain achieved during the 1960s and about 2/3 of the gain realized during the 1980s. A similar ranking obtains when the Real Per Capita GDP is used as the measure of well-being. The growth in Real Compensation during the 1990s is virtually identical with that of the 1980s. In both expansions the gains are small compared to the 1960s.

There are several reasons for the relative weak performance of the 1980s and 1990s. The first is related, in part, to the secular fall in the growth rate of labor productivity noted above. The average gain in labor productivity during the expansions of the 1980s and 1990s was less than 40% of the average achieved during the 1960s. The decline in productivity growth accounts for most of the difference in real per capita income growth. A second reason linked to the first, is the shallow nature of the 1990-91 downturn. A shallow downturn is unlikely to be followed by a recovery and expansion that has large cyclically related productivity gains. Now that productivity rates have risen, material well-being has improved more rapidly.

While not directly related to overall well-being, the distribution of income across income classes and the trend in the distribution over time is frequently of major interest to the citizens of a nation.[1]

Table 13. Measures of Material Well-Being

Expansion Years	Real Per-Capita GDP (1996 $)	Real Disposable Personal Income Per Capita (1996 $)	Real Compensation per Hour[a] (1992=100)
1992	$26,941	$20,320	100.0
1993	27,366	20.386	99.6
1994	28,195	20,711	99.5
1995	28,679	21,085	98.9
1996	30,465	22,138	99.3
1997	30,445	22,269	100.7
1998	31,474	23,359	104.5
Percentage Change	16.8%	15.0%	4.5%
1983	$21,904	$16,686	91.9
1984	23,293	17,803	92.1
1985	23,974	18,232	93.2
1986	24,568	18,644	96.3
1987	25,178	18,873	96.6
1988	25,991	19,525	97.4
1989	26,651	19,837	95.8
Percentage Change	21.7%	18.9%	4.2%
1962	$13,825	9,668	66.2
1963	14,217	9,889	67.6
1964	14,834	10,459	69.9
1965	15,586	10,967	71.0
1966	16,420	11,419	73.0
1967	16,649	11,778	75.0
1968	17,270	12,198	77.6
Percentage Change	24.9%	26.2%	17.2%

[a] In the non-farm business sector.
Source: Department of Labor

---

[1] For an additional discussion of this issue, see CRS Report RL30357, *The Distribution of*

In the post-World War II era (from 1947 to 1997), there appears to be some trend toward greater inequality in the distribution of income among families. The relevant data are shown in table 14. It is doubtful, however, if this shift is a cyclical phenomenon.

Table 14. Income Distribution among Families (data in percentages)

	Shares of Income Received by					
	Lowest fifth	Second fifth	Third fifth	Fourth fifth	Highest fifth	Top 5%
1998	4.2%	9.9%	15.7%	23.0%	47.3%	20.7%
1997	4.2	10.0	15.7	23.0	47.2	20.7
1996	4.2	10.0	15.8	23.1	46.8	20.3
1995	4.4	10.1	15.8	23.2	46.5	20.0
1994	4.4	10.0	15.7	23.3	46.9	20.1
1993	4.1	9.9	15.7	23.3	47.0	20.3
1992	4.3	10.5	16.5	24.0	44.7	17.6
1989	4.6%	10.6%	16.5%	23.7%	44.6%	17.9%
1988	4.6	10.7	16.7	24.0	44.0	17.2
1987	4.6	10.7	16.8	24.0	43.8	17.2
1986	4.7	10.9	16.9	24.1	43.4	16.5
1985	4.8	11.0	16.9	24.3	43.1	16.1
1984	4.8	11.1	17.1	24.5	42.5	15.4
1983	4.9	11.2	17.2	24.5	42.4	15.3
1968	5.6%	12.4%	17.7%	23.7%	40.5%	15.6%
1967	5.4	12.2	17.5	23.5	41.4	16.4
1966	5.6	12.4	17.8	23.8	40.5	15.6
1965	5.2	12.2	17.8	23.9	40.9	15.5
1964	5.1	12.0	17.7	24.0	41.2	15.9
1963	5.0	12.1	17.7	24.0	41.2	15.8
1962	5.0	12.1	17.6	24.0	41.3	15.7

Source: Bureau of Census

The percentage of income received by the lowest 60% of American families declined throughout the period 1962-1997. At the beginning of each expansion, the percentage received by this group was below that received during the sixth year of the previous long expansion. The percentage of income received by the fourth fifth of American families remained nearly constant at 23% to 24% of the total. For the top fifth of American families, the percent of income they received rose throughout these three expansions with the percentage received being higher at the start of each expansion than in the sixth year of the previous expansion (this is also almost true for the top 5% of families).[2]

---

[2] A shortcoming of this type of analysis is that families can move in the distribution. A family in the bottom 20% of the distribution in the 1960s need not be in that distribution during the 1980s and 1990s. This analysis does not track individual families. It merely consists of a ranking of families by income from lowest to highest. Thus, it may not be the case that the poor got poorer in the sense of individual families got worse off over time.

Chapter 8

FINANCIAL MARKET DEVELOPMENTS

Table 15 contains data on the nominal and estimated real interest yields on 90-day Treasury bills and 10-year Treasury bonds and the nominal and real rates of change of the Dow Jones and Standard and Poors 500 stock indexes.[1]

Estimates of real interest rates during the 1990s are quite a bit lower than during the 1980s and close to those during the 1960s (the short term rates are lower while the longer-term rates are comparable).

It is believed that the generally lower real rates during the 1990s compared with the 1980s are due to a smaller federal budget deficit relative to GDP. The decline in the budget deficit made a positive contribution to the national saving rate and, all else held constant, should have reduced real interest rates.

An interesting conclusion one might draw from this comparison is that real interest rates really tell us very little about economic expansions.[2] These three expansions occurred in environments of both low and high real rates.

---

[1] The real yields are calculated by subtracting the increase in the CPI for the year from the nominal interest yield on the debt securities and rate of change of the stock indexes. They are, thus, exposit real yields and rates of change.

[2] For a discussion of the role the stock market boom may play in the expansion of the 1990s, see CRS Report RL30518, *The Stock Market and The Economic Outlook*. By Brian W. Cashell, April 10, 2000.

Table 15. Financial Market Yields (data in percentages)

| | Stock Market Indices | | | | Treasury Securities | | | |
| | Dow Jones | | S&P 500 | | 90-Day T-Bills | | 10-Year Bonds | |
	Nominal	Real	Nominal	Real	Nominal	Real	Nominal	Real
1992	12.1%	9.1%	10.5%	7.5%	3.5%	0.5%	7.0%	4.0%
1993	7.2	4.2	8.6	5.6	3.0	0.0	5.9	2.9
1994	7.7	5.1	2.0	-0.6	4.3	1.7	7.1	4.5
1995	18.5	15.7	17.7	14.9	5.5	2.7	6.6	3.8
1996	27.8	24.8	23.8	20.8	5.0	2.0	6.4	3.4
1997	29.6	27.3	30.3	28.0	5.1	2.8	6.4	4.1
1998	15.9	14.3	24.3	22.7	4.8	3.2	5.3	3.7
Total Rise[a]	194.5%	146.0%	188.5%	141.1%				
1983	34.5%	31.3%	34.0%	30.8%	8.6%	5.4%	11.1%	7.9%
1984	-1.0	-5.3	0.0	-4.3	9.6	5.3	12.4	8.1
1985	12.7	9.1	16.4	12.8	7.5	3.9	10.6	7.0
1986	35.0	33.1	26.5	24.6	6.0	4.1	7.7	5.8
1987	27.0	23.4	21.4	17.8	5.8	2.2	8.4	4.8
1988	-9.5	-13.6	-7.3	-11.4	6.7	2.6	8.9	4.8
1989	21.7	16.9	21.5	16.7	8.1	3.3	8.5	3.7
Total Rise	183.7%	120.8%	169.7%	109.9%				
1962	-7.5%	-8.5%	-5.9%	-6.9%	2.8%	1.8%	4.0%	3.0%
1963	11.7	10.4	12.0	10.7	3.2	2.9	4.0	2.7

| | Stock Market Indices | | | | Treasury Securities | | | |
| | Dow Jones | | S&P 500 | | 90-Day T-Bills | | 10-Year Bonds | |
	Nominal	Real	Nominal	Real	Nominal	Real	Nominal	Real
1964	16.8	15.5	16.5	15.2	3.5	2.2	4.2	3.9
1965	9.2	7.6	8.4	6.8	4.0	2.4	4.3	2.5
1966	-4.1	-7.0	-3.3	-6.2	4.9	2.0	4.9	2.0
1967	0.6	-2.5	7.8	4.7	4.3	1.2	5.1	2.0
1968	3.1	-1.1	7.4	3.2	5.3	1.1	5.2	1.0
Total Rise	31.0%	12.6%	48.9%	27.9%				

[a] The real rise over each period is computed by taking the nominal index number divided by the CPI in the fifth year of each expansion and dividing it by a similar real index number in the year preceding the first year of expansion.

Source: Department of Treasury, the Dow Jones Industrial, and S&P 500.

Chapter 8

WHY DO ECONOMIC EXPANSIONS COME TO AN END?

That economic expansions come to an end is beyond dispute. The National Bureau of Economic Research, the nonpartisan, nonprofit organization that dates business cycles for the United States, has concluded that America has had nine completed economic expansions since the end of World War II. The expansion of the 1990s is the 10th.

Most observers believe that the proximate cause for the end of the nine completed expansions has been inflation. In their view the rate accelerated beyond what the Federal Reserve was willing to tolerate and restrictive monetary policy was applied.[1] Not only did the inflation rate fall, but the economic expansion peaked and a downturn ensued. The ultimate cause of downturns is, of course, more complex. In at least two expansions, both in the 1970s, the economy was suddenly hit by a major supply shock when, under the leadership of the OPEC oil cartel, would oil prices increased substantially. In other instances, however, the ultimate cause of the buildup of excess demand may have been due either to economic policies that, based on a miscalculation of a crucial parameter such as the value of the NAIRU. The implementation of policies based on these doctrines and computations may have led to the buildup of excess demand causing the inflation rate to rise. It is instructive, therefore, to look at the economic policies underpinning the long expansions of the 1960s and 1980s.

---

[1] In some cases, the Federal Reserve had little choice since the United States was linked to other trading countries by fixed exchange rates. Inflation poses special problems for such a regime. Whenever the U.S. inflation rate continued for any time above the rate posted by its trading partners, the dollar would tend to become overvalued leading to a growing trade deficit and the need for remedial action by the Federal Reserve.

THE 1960S

The economists that headed the Council of Economic Advisers (CEA) in the Kennedy-Johnson years, Walter Heller, Gardner Ackley, and Arthur Okun, had the view that the judicious use of fiscal policy, aggregate demand could be managed in such a way that the economy could be brought to full employment and then kept growing along a path consistent with the ability of the economy to supply additional output. Critical to this plan was the notion of full employment. And here the Council relied on the view that a fixed tradeoff existed between the unemployment rate and the rate of inflation (the so-called Phillips Curve).[2]

This tradeoff provided no unique measure of an unemployment rate consistent with full employment. Rather, based, in part, on recent historical experience, the Council selected an unemployment rate of 4% as its definition of full employment. This was regarded as an interim goal in the sense that it was believed that further reductions of the unemployment rate could be achieved only by innovative labor market policies designed to deal with what was thought to be structural problems, or problems that could not be addressed by further manipulations of aggregate demand.

Policy initiatives coming from the Administration supported this assessment. Principal among them was the Revenue Act of 1964, whose tax cuts were designed to stimulate demand and, in the sound bite of the day, "get America moving again." As the expansion continued, faith in the use of fiscal policy grew. By 1965 articles with titles such as "We Are All Keynesians Now" and "Why Recessions are Obsolete" began to appear in the national press.[3]

However, shortly after this tax cut took effect the U.S. became increasingly involved in Vietnam. The growing size of the military commitment and the effects of demand stimulation began to reduce the unemployment rate and by February 1966 it had fallen below 4%. To contain the developing inflationary pressures, the Council in 1967 urged a temporary 10% income tax surcharge.[4] The Administration introduced the proposal in

---

[2] For a discussion of this program, see *Annual Report of the Council of Economic Advisers.* January 1962, pp. 44-49, and Heller, Walter W. *New Dimensions of Political Economy.* Cambridge, Ma.: Harvard University Press. 1966.

[3] For the "We are All Keynesians Now," see *Time Magazine,* December 31, 1965 and for "Why Recessions are Obsolete," see *Nations Business,* May 1965.

[4] The CEA was clearly worried about the upward thrust of prices in 1966 – it found them rising at a "clearly unacceptable rate." It opined that if the unemployment rate could be held at its 1966 level, the rate of rise in prices would be substantially smaller in 1967.

January 1968 and it became law on June 28th (the Revenue and Control Act of 1968).

As the unemployment rate continued to fall (by September 1968 it had for the first time reached an expansion low of 3.5%) inflationary pressures grew. In the CEA view, the tax hike in 1968 was, unfortunately, too little too late. It expressed the opinion that the inflationary pressures that began to build in mid-1967 were too well established by the time the tax hike took effect to be cured quickly. In addition, a growing trade deficit caused dollar denominated liabilities abroad to build at an alarming rate threatening to force the United States to devalue the dollar. Ultimately, the Federal Reserve stepped in, applied the monetary brakes, the expansion peaked, and the economy then entered a downturn that lasted about a year (from December 1969 to November 1970). This did not, however, diminish the faith of many economists that had fiscal policy been applied in a timely fashion, the expansion could have been kept going for many additional months.

If the NAIRU concept that is now widely held by economists is correct, the Revenue Act of 1964 was not needed to provide additional demand stimulus. By 1962, the actual unemployment rate, 5.5%, was exactly the same as the CBO estimate of NAIRU for that year.[5] As the unemployment rate was pushed down by fiscal and monetary policies toward the target rate of 4%, the seeds were sown that ended the expansion. The enactment of the surtax in 1968 probably did little to change the situation. As long as 4% remained the targeted unemployment rate, the end result was accelerating inflation. Thus, an economic policy that is now regarded as questionable, may have been the ultimate reason why the expansion came to an end. It should, of course, be remembered, that economists had not yet come up with the concept of NAIRU. This was a theoretical development that came into vogue in the late 1960s based on the work of Professors Edmund Phelps and Milton Friedman.[6]

THE 1980S

The economic expansion that got under way at the end of 1982 was preceded by a massive cut in taxes embodied in the Economic Recovery Tax

---

[5] Alternative measures of the NAIRU are available.

[6] While the NAIRU had not yet been formulated, there was a belief held by a good number of economists that money was neutral in its effects on such variables as employment and the flow of output. The Phillips curve, implying a permanent tradeoff between inflation (a money driven phenomenon) and the unemployment rate is inconsistent with monetary neutrality.

Act of 1981. While there is little doubt that this fiscal package had a large initial effect on aggregate demand, it was claimed that the reduction in marginal income tax rates and various business taxes would, by increasing the incentives to work, save, and add to capital, have a major effect on boosting the growth of aggregate supply. Substantiating these claims has proved more difficult.[7]

Monetary policy, freed during the 1970s from the need to maintain a fixed exchange rate, could now concentrate on getting the economy to full employment and keeping it growing along a path characterized by full employment and low inflation.

Success was achieved in the sense that the unemployment rate continued to fall throughout the expansion. By 1985, Secretary of the Treasury James Baker felt confident enough to state: "I don't think that we have to accept the fact that there will be these [business] cycles in the future." *The Wall Street Journal* summarized Secretary Bakers' testimony by saying that: "...with proper fiscal and monetary policies, there isn't any reason the expansion can't continue indefinitely."[8]

As the expansion continued, the ardor of the national press proclaiming the new economic era was upon us was dampened by the stock market crash of October 1987. In terms of timing and the relative magnitude of the decline in stock prices, it nearly exactly paralleled the great crash of October 1929. What seems to have surprised the press was that the country did not dip into recession. Indeed, the expansion continued on for several additional years. However, between 1987 and 1988, the actual unemployment rate fell below the NAIRU. The CBO measure of NAIRU (January 2000) is 6.0% for 1987 and 5.9% for both 1988 and 1989 while the actual unemployment rates for those years is 6.2%, 5.5%, and 5.3% (the 5.3% rate continued to prevail through mid-1990).

It is interesting that the CEA had integrated the notion of NAIRU into its formulation of policy. In the February 1990 *Report*, it states:

The design of sound economic policies depends on the level of the NAIRU.

It then goes on to add:

---

[7] The initial demand-side stimulus from this tax cut package was substantial. The standardized or full employment measure of the federal budget deficit rose from –0.5% of GDP in 1981 to –4.8% in 1986 (as calculated by CBO-January 2000).

[8] For Secretary Bakers' testimony, see The Federal Budget for 1986. Hearings Before the Committee on Appropriations, House of Representatives. Ninety-ninth Congress, First Session. Washington, D.C.: U.S. Government Printing Office, 1985, and *Wall Street Journal*. February 26, 1985.

Unfortunately, the NAIRU is not observable...But a rough estimate of the current level can be inferred from recent trends in the unemployment rate and in wage inflation.

And, after some discussion, concludes:

Thus, the average rate of unemployment in 1989 – 5.3 percent – may not be far above the non-accelerating inflation rate of unemployment. (Italics in the original).

Unfortunately, for policy purposes, the NAIRU in 1989, 5.9% (as calculated by CBO-January 2000), was more than 0.5% above the then prevailing unemployment rate of 5.3%. And, in conformance with teachings of theory, the inflation rate began to accelerate. The CPI rose 1.1% in 1986, 4.4% in both 1987 and 1988, 4.6% in 1989, and 6.1% in 1990.[9]

Since the CEA believed that the prevailing unemployment was above the NAIRU, it had some difficulty explaining the acceleration in the inflation rate. In its Report for 1991, it concluded:

The downturn was caused in large part by the economic effects of Iraq's invasion of Kuwait. That caused a jump in oil prices and directly reduced business and consumer confidence. These factors, coupled with continuing uncertainty about the timing of the resolution of the crisis, dealt a substantial blow to an economy already sluggish from other factors. These included worldwide increases in interest rates, unexpectedly tight credit conditions, and the lingering effects of a tightening of monetary policy from early 1988 through mid-1989that was undertaken in a successful attempt to prevent an increase in inflation (page 87).

Thus, the CEA assigned a major role in the downturn to the Iraqi invasion of Kuwait. Unfortunately, the National Bureau of Economic Research dates the peak of the 1980s expansion as occurring in July of 1990, a month before Iraq seized Kuwait. It would appear from this dating, that Federal Reserve policy played the major role in the downturn, a policy necessitated by a rising rate of inflation. And a case can be made that the inflation rate accelerated because the unemployment rate that prevailed for two years was below the NAIRU. A crucial parameter estimate had been mistakenly made.

---

[9] The rate of increase in the CPI is measured on a December over December basis. The low rate of increase in 1986 was heavily influenced by the sharp fall in oil prices following the break-up of the international oil cartel.

THE 1990S

As the expansion of the 1990s has continued, it has given rise to a view in the press that is supported by the business community, that it has the possibility of continuing indefinitely. The business view was directed, in part, against those policies that it saw as restraining aggregate demand growth.[10] According to the business view, pessimistic assessments of productivity growth by the Federal Reserve, and thus, the growth in potential GDP, was about to lead the Fed to restrict the growth of money and credit and, thus, aggregate demand. According to the business community, higher productivity growth had taken place based on increased efficiency forced on firms by the "globalization of business" and the revolution in information technology typified by the widespread use of fax machines, cellular telephones, personal computers, modems, and the Internet. These same forces were also holding down the inflation rate making it possible to reduce the unemployment rate far below the then prevailing estimate of the NAIRU. In fact, the financial press, support by an assortment of economists, called for the scrapping of an economic stabilization program based on the NAIRU. Thus, as the nation's financial press saw things, the nation's prosperity was being undermined by policymakers guided by incorrect policies.

More disconcerting for the continuation of the expansion is the emergence of a possible conflict over stabilization policy, even though the policymakers are in agreement over the goals of that policy. The Council of Economic Advisers continues to accept the NAIRU as an appropriate way to view full employment, even though they caution that it is subject to various measurement problems and is not to be regarded as a constant. It is worth repeating the CEA view of the NAIRU from its 1999 *Report*:

> *Although the NAIRU is an indicator of the risk of inflation, estimates of the NAIRU have a wide band of uncertainty and should be used carefully in formulating policy. The NAIRU implicit in the Administration's forecast has drifted down in recent years and is now within a range centered on 5.3 percent.[11]*

Since the actual unemployment rate has been below 5.3% since February 1997, one should have expected some acceleration in the inflation rate. That this has not yet occurred, the Council attributes to special factors

---

[10] For a more extensive discussion and evaluation of this view, see *The New Economic Paradigm: Is It New and Is It a Paradigm?* Op. Cit.

[11] It its 2000 *Report*, the NAIRU has been lowered to 5.2%.

(the fall in petroleum prices, the decline in import prices, technical changes related to the computation of the inflation rate). In its 2000 *Report* the Council opines that the NAIRU itself may have fallen dramatically in the late 1990s due to such factors as spare manufacturing capacity, new efficiencies in the labor market from the expanded use of temporary help workers and Internet job search resources, higher-than-expected productivity growth, and other things. Had these special factors not occurred, the inflation rate would have registered some mild acceleration.

The nation's central banker, Alan Greenspan, has stated in testimony that he does not find the NAIRU to be a useful concept. Rather, he views tightness in the labor markets, a precursor of potential inflationary pressures, as governed by the "pool of available workers." This group is composed of the unemployed and people who are not now at work, but who would like a job.[12] The Greenspan view of the potential labor supply suggests that the economy could continue to run at an actual unemployment rate substantially below the current estimate of the NAIRU. How this potential conflict will play out remains to be seen. How it does play out may well determine whether the expansion of the 1990s continues well into the 21st century.

---

[12] Mr. Greenspan has given no precise definition of this group, but in addition to the unemployed, it probably consists of people who are not now in the labor force, but who would accept a job if an appropriate one came to their attention, and individuals who are forced to work part-time because they cannot find a full time job. See also CRS Report RL30283, *The Unemployment Rate and the Potential Supply of Labor.* By Linda Levine, August 16, 1999.

Chapter 9

CONCLUSION

The on-going economic expansion that began in March 1991 has entered the history books as the longest expansion in American history. A comparison of this expansion with the expansion of the 1960s and the long expansion of the 1980s, which, at 92 months, is the third longest in U.S. history, yields many interesting insights. The comparisons made in this study utilize the first 48 months of data for these three expansions.

It is well to bear in mind that the depth of the recession that preceded these three expansions was quite different. In particular, the downturn that preceded the expansion of the 1980s was the deepest since the Great Depression of 1929-32. Some of the comparisons are conditioned by this difference.

The growth of GDP over each expansion is one companion that depends, in part, on the severity of the preceding downturn. From this perspective, it is not surprising that GDP growth during the 1990s was the weakest of the three expansions given the shallow and short duration of the contraction that preceded it. However, also relevant to this comparison is productivity growth for this and the growth of the labor force are the two major determinants of GDP growth over the longer run, once full employment is achieved. And, in the area of productivity growth, the expansions of the 1980s and 1990s lag behind the 1960s. Productivity growth in both of these expansions was a little less than 40% of the average productivity growth achieved during the 1960s. However, spending for capital goods (or investment spending) has played an important role in the expansion of the 1990s as it did during the 1960s. This may be important in raising productivity in the future. There is a growing consensus that some of the productivity increases of recent years are linked to this investment.

This slowdown in productivity growth has profoundly affected the growth in the material well-being of Americans. Depending on the measures of material well-being used, per capita increases during the 1990s were only from 20% to 33% as large as the per capita gains realized in the 1960s (the 1980s are, using two of the three measures, slightly better than the 1990s). This slowdown in the growth of per capita well-being has also been accompanied by a shift in the distribution of income among families towards greater inequality, although this shift does not appear to be cyclical.

The decline in labor force growth during the 1990s has raised the median age of the work force back to what it had been in the 1960s. A more mature work force is supposedly conducive to enhanced labor productivity and could be a factor in explaining why the rate of growth of that productivity has risen in the last few years. It is atypical when compared to the mature years of previous expansions.

With the slowdown in labor force growth in the 1990s has come a slowdown in the growth rate at which women participate in the labor force and a slowdown in the rate at which men are withdrawing from participating in the labor force. The labor force participation rate of women in the 1990s was about 50% higher than during the 1960s.

Job creation during the 1990s was heavily concentrated in the service sector as it was during the 1980s. Very few jobs during both of these expansions were added in manufacturing. This was not the case during the 1960s. In part, this reflects the way Americans are spending their incomes. A growing fraction of which is spent on services and nondurables. Also relevant is the growing openness of the U.S. economy. The foreign trade sector, measured as the sum of exports and imports, rose to nearly 30% of GDP in the 1990s as opposed to a high of about 10% in the late 1960s (this increase in openness may help explain the secular trend toward greater inequality in the distribution of income**Error! Bookmark not defined.** among families).

The inflation performance of the 1990s compares favorably with the expansion of the 1960s except that during the latter the inflation rate accelerated as the expansion matured. During the 1990s, the pattern has been for the rate to decelerate.

The investor who bought either the Dow Jones Industrial average of the S&P 500 would have had the largest nominal and real gains during the 1990s. The cumulative real gains during the 1990s were nearly 11 times larger for the Dow Jones and 5 times larger for the S&P 500 than during the 1960s (the gains during the 1980s were close to those of the 1990s). The

1980s and 1990s were clearly a kind of golden age for those who held common stock.

The unemployment rate during the 1960s was the lowest of the three expansions. The 1990s rate has been lower than that achieved during the 1980s. In all three expansions, the unemployment rate achieved by the seventh year of the expansion was well below measures of full employment based on the NAIRU concept. Thus, if the NAIRU is the correct way to measure full employment, one can argue that the seeds for the end of each expansion were sown early on. We know that the expansion of the 1960s and 1980s did end. As of the date of this report the fate of the expansion of the 1990s is not yet evident.

Chapter 10

EPILOGUE

The comparisons made in the body of this book utilized data from the first 84 months of each of the three expansions, since the expansion of the 1980s expired soon thereafter. This was not true of the two other expansions. The expansion of the 1960s continued for nearly two more years while the current expansion is still going strong more than two years after passing the 84-month benchmark. The purpose of the epilogue is to continue the comparison of these two expansions for two additional years: 1969-70 and 1999-2000. The data used for the comparisons are in Table 16.

Table 16. Comparing the Expansions

	1969	1970	1999	2000 (forecast)
Economic Growth	3.0%	0.2%	4.2%	5.2%
Labor Productivity Growth	0.5%	2.0%	3.1%	3.9%
Unemployment	3.5%	5.0%	4.2%	4.0%
Inflation (CPI)	5.5%	5.7%	2.2%	3.2%
Investment (as % of GDP)	13.1%	12.2%	18.8%	18.7%
Combined Budget Deficit (-)	0.3%	-0.3%	1.4%	3.4%
Net Exports (as % of GDP)	-2.0%	-1.8%	-3.6%	-4.5%
Total Trade (as % of GDP)	10.0%	10.7%	26.9%	25.4%
Yield on 90-Day T-Bills (Real)	1.2%	0.8%	2.5%	2.6%
S&P 500 Rate of Return (Nominal)	-0.9%	-14.9%	20.1%	11.5%

Source: Historical data from NIPA, BLS, CBO; forecasts from DRI, August 2000.
Note: Combined Budget Deficit refers to the sum of the on-budget and off-budget deficits.

The most notable difference between this period of the two expansions is that the expansion of the 1960s was coming to an end as the economy overheated and the Fed was forced to tighten monetary policy in response. As we noted above, the cause for the overheating may well have been the selection of policymakers of an inappropriate unemployment goal (assuming that the NAIRU is an appropriate measure of full employment). Nevertheless, by 1970 GDP growth was falling, both the unemployment and inflation rates were rising as was trade deficit, the budget was moving from surplus to deficit, and productivity growth was slowing.

The 1990s expansion, by contrast, appears to be getting a second wind. On the positive side, the growth rates of GDP and productivity are accelerating, the unemployment rate continues to fall, and the budget surplus continues to grow as a fraction of GDP. On the side of concerns, the inflation rate is moving up a little (but this may be temporary and due to special factors) and the trade deficit is now running in excess of 4% of GDP (the highest in 40 years).

ECONOMIC GROWTH

During the final two years of the expansion of the 1960s, GDP growth fell noticeably (see Table 1). In six of the first seven years of that expansion, GDP grew in excess of 4% (in three of these years, it was 6% or higher). In the final year of that expansion, GDP hardly grew at all. This is not true of the expansion of the 1990s. Since 1995, GDP growth has been strong – in excess of 3.5% per year. This is expected to continue through 2000. (Over the first half of the year, GDP grew at an annualized rate of 5%.) Moreover, although some economists believe that GDP growth must slow somewhat from its current pace for the expansion to be sustainable, there is evidence that GDP growth could continue in the 3% to 4% range for some time into the future. While this growth rate would be lower than we have enjoyed in the past few years, it would still be substantially higher than the average growth rate, 2.8%, for the 1974-1995 period.

PRODUCTIVITY

A key factor in determining the long run sustainable rate of GDP growth is the growth rate of productivity. The behavior of productivity during the 1960s corresponds to the typical pattern expected from economic theory: the growth rate tends to fall as the expansion continues (see Table 9). The pattern during the 1990s is quite different. In the first year of the expansion, the growth rate was high, but then it fell sharply and remained low for three years. Then, beginning in 1995, the growth rate began to rise. At first, the rise was regarded as a temporary phenomenon. But not only has the higher rate persisted; it has accelerated and appears to be on a more sustainable course. This behavior has been attributed to the high proportion of the increase in GDP accounted for by investment, especially in PCs, data processing equipment, and the like.[1] For some observers, this increase in productivity growth harkens back to the golden age of productivity that characterized the years from the end of World War II until the end of the 1960s.[2]

THE STATE OF PUBLIC FINANCES

The state of the federal budget provides another contrast between this period of the two expansions. Under the stress of the Vietnam War, the deficit in the federal budget began to move upward in 1966 (see Table 6). It was temporarily pushed into a one-year surplus in 1969 after Congress passed the 10% income tax surcharge in 1968. This tax increase had a dampening effect on aggregate demand that probably contributed to the expansion ending when it did. But the tax increase may have been unavoidable since the government had been accumulating debt at an unsustainable pace since 1966. By 1980, the budget moved back into deficit, where it would remain until 1998. The history of the 1990s is quite different. The budget deficit as a percentage of GDP continued to decline throughout the expansion. By 1998, the budget was in surplus for the first time since 1969. This trend has continued as the budget has not only been in surplus for 1999 and 2000, but the surplus as a percentage of GDP has been rising (and the trend is projected to continue).[3]

---

[1] It should be noted from Table 16, that an equally high proportion of GDP growth during the 1960s was also accounted for by investment spending. Yet this did not sustain the growth rate of productivity. In fact, the secular decline in the growth of productivity that persisted until the mid-1990s may have started in the late 1960s.

[2] For more information, see US Library of Congress, Congressional Research Service, *The US Long-Term Growth Rate. Has it Increased?* by Craig Elwell, CRS Report RS20608, June 21, 2000.

[3] It should e noted that this increasing surplus serves as a break on the growth in aggregate demand and, thus, helps to keep the economy from overheating.

UNEMPLOYMENT

The 1960s are regarded as the golden era for low unemployment in the post-World War II era. In 1968 the rate had declined to 3.6%, an unemployment rate that would not be reached again in the period covered by this study. The military draft and the war in Vietnam were responsible in large measure for this result. Large numbers of young males, a group that normally have relatively high unemployment rates, were taken into military service. Nevertheless, as the expansion came to an end in 1970, the unemployment rate moved up to 5%.

The unemployment experience of the 1990s tracks in large measure that of the 1960s. The unemployment rate has fallen from an average of 7.4% during 1992 to an average of 4% during the first half of 2000, and this was done without a war and military conscription.

While the actual unemployment rate during both periods is of interest for many reasons, economists are concerned about the sustainable rate of unemployment. This is commonly measured by the NAIRU. Should the actual unemployment rate dip below the NAIRU, economic theory suggests that the inflation rate should accelerate and, an accelerating rate of inflation is often the trigger for policy intervention that bring expansions to an end. Computations by CBO (January 2000) suggest that over the course of the 1960s, the NAIRU rose from a low of 5.5% in 1962 to a high of 5.9% in 1970. Since the actual unemployment rate was pushed to 3.5% in 1969, NAIRU-based theories predict that the inflation rate should have accelerated. It did and the expansion was brought to an end by a tightening of monetary policy by the Federal Reserve.

During the 1990s, the NAIRU is also thought to have fallen because of favorable changes in the labor market. The CEA now pegs the rate at about 5.2% (a similar estimate is held by CBO). Since the actual unemployment is far below this, we should again expect the inflation rate to accelerate. Thus far, this has not happened. Nevertheless, it suggests that the U.S. is now producing output at a rate in excess of full employment, a situation that is not thought to be sustainable.

INFLATION

A major reason why economic expansions come to an end is an accelerating inflation rate. Indeed, this is what ultimately brought the expansion of the 1960s to an end. As that expansion continued, the inflation rate rose steadily (see Table 12). By 1968 it was above 4% and climbing. It accelerated to 5.5% in 1969 and 5.7% in 1970. This pattern is not present in the 1990s. In fact, quite the reverse. The inflation rate decelerated over the period 1992-1998. While the rate was higher in 1999 and is expected to be a little higher during 2000, it is still only about half as large as during 1970. However, part of the reason for this experience is attributable to special factors, notably a fall in petroleum and other import prices. Some of these have since reversed themselves and some acceleration in the rate may now be expected especially because the current unemployment rate is far below the NAIRU and has been below that rate for several years. Most threatening, oil prices have risen from a 30-year low in 1998 to a 15-year high in 2000.[4]

GLOBALIZATION

A great difference between the 1960s and the 1990s is the degree of globalization. The sum of imports and exports was less than 10% of GDP during the 1960s. This sum is now 2 ½ times as large and growing. The U.S. is now a far more open economy than it was in the 1960s. However, as both expansions matured, they faced growing current account deficits. During the first half of 2000 the current-account deficit has run in excess of 4% of GDP, more than twice as large as the deficits of 1969-1970.

While some economists regard the large and growing current account deficits of the current expansion as a source of potential instability, others do not share this belief. A deficit in the current account, measured as the difference between exports and imports, must be offset by a surplus in the capital account, measured as the difference between foreign capital entering the US and US capital going abroad. Thus, it may be that the current-account deficits have risen because foreign investors want to buy American assets because of the favorable economic outlook. So long as they do, the U.S. will have to have a current-account deficit. In other words, the current-account deficit is a direct result of the capital-account surplus rather than the opposite, a sign of strength not weakness.[5] The trade deficits of the 1960s expansion resulted in large measure from the need to maintain a large

---

[4] For more information, see US Library of Congress, Congressional Research Service, *Rising Oil Prices: What Dangers Do They Pose for the Economy?* by Marc Labonte, CRS report RL30634, August 15, 2000.

[5] For more information, see US Library of Congress, Congressional Research Service, *America's Growing Current-Account Deficit: Its Cause and What It Means for the Economy* by Gail Makinen, CRS report RL30534, April 19, 2000.

military establishment in Vietnam, not because America offered a favorable climate for foreign investment, and were a source of potential instability.[6]

FINANCIAL MARKETS

During 1969 and 1970, asset markets performed poorly as investors reacted to the impending economic downturn and the remedial action by the Federal Reserve that brought this about. The S&P 500 Index, which offers a good estimate of how the stocks of large firms perform, showed a slightly negative return for 1969 and a larger negative in return in 1970. This is not the case during 1999 and 2000. In 1999, the S&P rose in excess of 20% and in 2000 it is forecast to rise in excess of 10%.[7] In both expansions, nominal yields on federal debt have tended to rise, but during 1969-70 that rise did

---

[6] Without entering into an extensive discussion of this matter, the instability of the trade deficits of the 1960s arose because the U.S. maintained fixed exchange rates with foreign countries. The trade deficits were financed by an accumulation of dollar liabilities abroad. It was feared that if these became too large, foreign central banks would ask for their conversion into gold, as ultimately happened. As a result, the United States was forced during the 1970s first to devalue the dollar and then allow the dollar to float in foreign exchange markets. The current system of flexible exchange rates traces its origin to this period. While the current regime of floating exchange rates exposes the US to volatility risk, it is less likely to result in crises like the US suffered in the 1970s because of their fixed exchange rate regime.

[7] *Blue Chip Survey of Forecasters*, June 2000.

not keep pace with the rate of inflation and *ex post* real yields fell. During 1999-2000, real yields have tended to rise.[8]

---

[8] Rising real yields have often been interpreted as a sign that the Federal Reserve is tightening monetary policy while falling real yields have been regarded as a sign of easing. While this is a possible interpretation, it is not the only one since interest rates are determined by both supply and demand. Thus, a rising real yield is consistent with a large demand for funds of the type produced by vigorous economic growth while a falling or low real rate is consistent with weak demand produced by recessions. Thus, the real rate by itself tells us little about the posture of monetary policy.

Chapter 11

SUMMARY

Towards the end of the decade, the expansion of the 1960s showed clear signs of overheating. Unemployment and inflation were rapidly rising, growth was falling, and the current-account deficit was widening. Government deficits were structural and the investment climate was poor. By contrast, at a similar point in the expansion that started in the 1990s, the rate of economic growth is still accelerating. Recent improvements in productivity suggest that the strong economic growth the US is currently enjoying may be sustainable although the expansion is already the longest in our history. If fiscal policy is not altered, government finances look set on a deficit-free path in the medium term.

But there are some troubling economic signs as well that could contain the seeds of the expansion's end. Unemployment is so low that it seems unlikely that future economic growth can be fueled by increases in the labor supply, as happened throughout the 1990s. The headline inflation rate has risen about 3%, and will prompt a further tightening of monetary policy if it does not fall soon. Investment remains reliant on foreign capital, as reflected in the record-high current-account deficit. Rising oil prices were prominent in the last three recessions (1974, 1980, 1991), although they have had little effect on economic growth to date in 2000.

INDEX